HOUSTON DECO

HOUSTON DECO

Modernistic Architecture of the Texas Coast

Jim Parsons & David Bush

Foreword by Madeleine McDermott Hamm

BRIGHT SKY PRESS

BRIGHT SKY PRESS

Box 416
Albany, Texas 76430

10 9 8 7 6 5 4 3 2 1

Library of Congress Cataloging-in-Publication Data

Parsons, Jim, 1977–
   Houston deco : modernistic architecture of the Texas coast / by Jim Parsons & David Bush ; foreword by Madeleine McDermott Hamm.
      p. cm.
   Includes bibliographical references and index.
   ISBN 978-1-933979-06-9 (jacketed hardcover : alk. paper) – ISBN 978-1-933979-07-6 (softcover with flaps : alk. paper) 1. Art deco (Architecture)—Texas—Houston. 2. Architecture—Texas—Houston—20th century. 3. Houston (Tex.)—Buildings, structures, etc. I. Bush, David, 1957– II. Title.

NA735.H68P37 2007
720.9764'1411—dc22

                                                  2007027765

Book and cover design by Isabel Lasater Hernandez
Edited by Dixie Nixon

Printed in China through Asia Pacific Offset

Photo page 2: Ceiling medallion, Alabama Theater, 1939
Opposite page: Lobby ceiling, Gulf Building, 1929

Step-back detail,
Petroleum Building,
1927

Opposite page:
Lantern, Chambers
County Courthouse,
1936

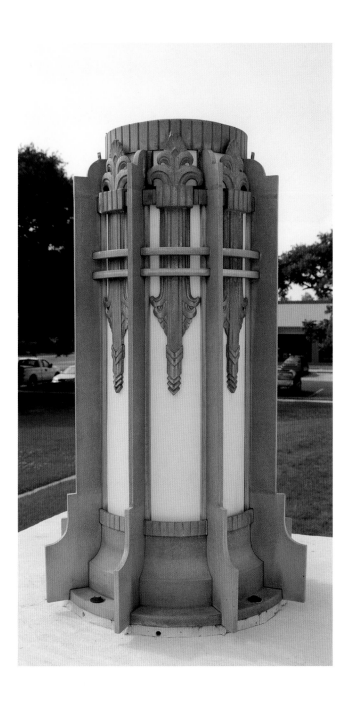

CONTENTS

PREFACE

In the summer of 2006, Greater Houston Preservation Alliance announced that the organization was adding three significant Art Deco properties to its Endangered Buildings List: the 1937 River Oaks Community Center, 1939 River Oaks Theater and 1939 Alabama Theater. The resulting media coverage and outpouring of public support for preserving these local landmarks marked a turning point in Houston's historic preservation movement.

In support of the organization's mission to increase awareness and appreciation of Houston's historic architecture, GHPA volunteer Jim Parsons and GHPA Programs and Information Director David Bush set out to document the city's modernistic architecture. What was supposed to be a project of several weeks grew to several months as the two worked, largely on their own time, to photograph and research buildings in Houston and surrounding communities. Their efforts resulted in this book, *Houston Deco*, and the Web site *www.HoustonDeco.org*.

Houston Deco is the third book published under GHPA's auspices since the organization was founded in 1978; it is the organization's first book to focus solely on 20th century architecture. The members, volunteers and staff of Greater Houston Preservation Alliance are grateful to the Houston Architecture Foundation and the Strake Foundation for supporting GHPA's efforts to bring this information to the widest possible audience.

This project integrates education, advocacy and committed action, the three concepts at the heart of GHPA's mission. The publication of *Houston Deco* is another important step toward achieving our goal of creating a preservation ethic for Houston.

—*Ramona Davis, Executive Director*
Greater Houston Preservation Alliance

Opposite page:
East entrance,
Houston City Hall,
1939

Foley's (now Macy's),
1947

FOREWORD

If Art Deco had not emerged in 1925 in Paris at the *Exposition Internationale des Arts Décoratifs et Industriels Modernes,* the then-new style probably would have been born in Houston.

Like Art Deco and Art Moderne, the sleeker style of the '30s, Houston was (and is) a forward-looking city, ready to embrace and advance the newest, freshest ideas. Art Deco turned away from the traditional motifs of the past—the classic urns, the gargoyles, the romantic swags and acanthus leaves—and replaced them with more angular, geometric designs. Then came streamlined images of the machine age, representing strength, speed and power.

It was the 20th century, the modern age of racy-looking cars, fast trains, grand ocean liners and airplanes. Elaborate movie palaces showed handsome couples at night clubs, dancing and dining in a Hollywood world, witty and sophisticated.

It was a time of excitement, discovery, adventure and promise.

Houston and Art Deco belonged together. Fresh and bold, both looked to the future, not toward the past.

Houston was a vibrant, young city poised for prominence. Visionary leaders such as Jesse H. Jones—banker, builder, publisher of the *Houston Chronicle* and political force—commissioned some of the city's most significant buildings in this new architectural style that makes them stand out today as historical treasures.

Even legendary Houston residential architect John F. Staub, who never saw a traditional style he couldn't adapt and improve on, succumbed to the sensuousness of the Moderne style in the 1937 River Oaks house he designed for Mr. and Mrs. Robert D. Straus (see *The Architecture of John F. Staub: Houston and the South* by Howard Barnstone, 1979, University of Texas Press).

Then, as today, Houston has forged its own style—not Southern, not Midwestern, not Western. Totally Texan, totally independent, playing by its own rules. At times that

Houston Municipal
Airport, 1940

Trips to Houston meant seeing the old Houston Municipal Airport Terminal, the grand downtown movie palaces, the imposing Gulf Building, the glamorous Shamrock Hotel, the River Oaks Shopping Center, Jeff Davis Hospital, the Coliseum with Roy Rogers and Dale Evans riding around the arena to shake outstretched young hands, Krupp & Tuffly where we bought new clothes for my first year at college. Who knew back then!

But as I studied design periods and styles in both architecture and furniture for my role as home design editor of the *Houston Chronicle,* I gained understanding and appreciation for all of them—from Queen Anne to mid-

independence has led to the loss of some of the early 20th century structures that told the story of Houston's "coming out" years when the foundation was being laid for the dynamic international city of today.

Still, our cityscape is punctuated with many striking examples of that early modern architecture. I can't remember when I first discovered, and subsequently fell in love with, Art Deco.

Looking back, I realize I grew up with many Deco landmarks, starting with the splashy marquee of the Showboat Theater in my hometown of Texas City, the marvelous Martini movie house in Galveston and the breathtaking San Jacinto Monument.

Shamrock Hotel, 1949

century—but felt strongly drawn to Art Deco.

Even now, I am thrilled by the incredible Deco motifs of the amazing interior details—the grillwork, the doors, the banking lobby ceiling—of the JPMorgan Chase Building, originally known as the Gulf Building. To borrow a familiar saying: "They just don't build them like that anymore!" All the more reason we must treasure them and save them.

—Madeleine McDermott Hamm

Madeleine McDermott Hamm is the *Houston Chronicle*'s former longtime Home Design Editor. She is now a freelance design writer and antiques dealer, and serves on the Board of Directors of Greater Houston Preservation Alliance. She was the writing partner of interior designer

Community Center, River Oaks, Houston, Texas

PHOTO BY BOB BAILEY   8A-H2556

Bill Stubbs on his 2004 book, *I Hate Red, You're Fired!* and his upcoming book, *A Moment of Luxury: Discovering the Beauty Around You*. She is an avid Houston Astros fan who attended the first and last Astros games played in the Astrodome, the world's first domed stadium; she is passionate about the Dome's preservation.

River Oaks Community Center, 1937

Gulf Building, 1929

INTRODUCTION

The Gulf Building symbolizes my conception of the Houston of Today. Both are essentially modern.

—Jesse H. Jones
July 29, 1929

T he opening of the 36-story Gulf Building in July 1929 marked the high point of the Roaring '20s construction boom that was transforming Houston. For many in the city, this distinctive Art Deco skyscraper symbolized their community's future.

Although modernistic architecture, which encompasses Art Deco and Art Moderne design, arrived in Houston comparatively late in the 1920s, it came at a critical time in the city's development. Houston was beginning its transition from medium-sized Southern city to major American metropolis. Modernistic architecture's growing popularity coincided with a conscious effort by Houston's business and civic leaders to tie the city's image to the American West and de-emphasize its Southern heritage.

Prior to 1927, most architect-designed buildings in Houston were either local versions of classical revival architecture or Victorian designs adapted for the city's hot, humid climate. The changes brought about by the arrival of modernistic architecture are clearly illustrated by the two tallest buildings constructed in Houston in the 1920s. The Niels Esperson Building (1927) is covered with detailing inspired by classical architecture, while the Gulf Building is comparatively

Niels Esperson Building, 1927

austere. Despite these differences, modernistic buildings did not completely break with the past. The Gulf Building is influenced by Gothic design and many of the city's Art Deco buildings exhibit stylized versions of classical architectural details.

Art Deco and Art Moderne

Most modernistic buildings in Houston exhibit elements of both Art Deco and Art Moderne design. There are very few textbook examples of either style in the city.

Art Deco

The classic angular design of the 1920s, sometimes called Zigzag Moderne, is seen most often on commercial and government buildings. Skyscrapers of the period often exhibit Art Deco details.

- Stucco is used to create smooth wall surfaces, although brick is also common in Houston, especially on apartment and commercial buildings. Cordova Shell limestone is used frequently to surface major government buildings in Texas.
- The façade is usually symmetrical.

Detail, Weingarten's Food Market No. 11, 1930

- Angular geometric forms such as zigzags and chevrons are used as decorative elements. Stylized sculpture and bas-relief panels are seen frequently on major public buildings.
- Pylons, towers and other projections above the roofline give Art Deco buildings their vertical orientation. Metals such as

aluminum and nickel are used to create elaborate grilles, plaques and other decorative elements. Metal ornamentation marking entryways is particularly ornate.

Art Moderne

Influenced by the sweeping lines of 1930s industrial design, Art Moderne reflects the era's fascination with streamlined ocean liners, locomotives and airplanes. As a result, the style is often called Streamline Moderne. Most Art Moderne buildings in Houston are commercial and industrial structures, although the style's impact can also be seen in the design of a few private homes.

- Art Moderne buildings usually have flat roofs and smooth wall surfaces covered with stucco.
- The façade is usually asymmetrical.
- Small ledges at the roofline and horizontal grooves or lines in the walls accentuate the horizontal orientation of Art Moderne buildings.
- One or more corners of the building are rounded.
- Windows are often continuous around corners. Glass block is used frequently and often covers whole sections of wall. Small round windows are also common.
- Stainless steel is used to create streamlined banisters, signage and decorative elements.

Local Architects

Alfred C. Finn and Joseph Finger, the most prominent and prolific Houston architects of the period, were responsible individually for several significant modernistic buildings. Finn, the principal architect on the

Detail, River Oaks Community Center expansion, 1948

Gulf Building, created restrained Art Deco designs for banker/developer/publisher Jesse H. Jones. Finger created more exuberant buildings for a variety of private clients, including the local Weingarten grocery chain. During the Great Depression, both Finn and Finger received important federally-funded commissions that resulted in significant modernistic buildings, including Finger's Houston City Hall and Finn's San Jacinto Monument. The two architects collaborated on the now-demolished Jefferson Davis Hospital. Another of Finn's large public projects, the Sam Houston Coliseum and Music Hall, has also been razed. After World War II, as other Houston architects embraced the International Style or adapted the tenets of Frank Lloyd Wright, Finn continued to create modified modernistic designs. His conservative approach attracted major clients into the 1950s, when he designed the Sakowitz Bros. Department Store on Main Street and the Ezekiel W. Cullen Building on the University of Houston campus.

Other significant architects of the period include Kenneth Franzheim, whose work on the Gulf Building helped bring modernistic architecture to prominence in Houston. Wyatt C. Hedrick created a significant body of modernistic designs; his most celebrated creation, the Shamrock Hotel, has been demolished. Moore & Lloyd created refined interpretations of Art Moderne design for commercial clients. Lamar Q. Cato specialized almost exclusively in school buildings, including several for the fledgling University of Houston. Even John Staub, who established his reputation designing elegant homes in a variety of revival styles, and William Ward Watkin, best known for his neo-Gothic churches and his work on the Rice University campus, tried their hands at modernistic design.

In Beaumont, 90 miles east of Houston, talented local architects created a unique collection of classic modernistic buildings. Former Beaumont mayor Fred C. Stone partnered with Louisiana native Augustin Babin to design the Jefferson County Courthouse, a landmark 14-story Art Deco skyscraper. Stone's later work included collaborations on the Art Deco First National Bank of Beaumont and Art Moderne White

House Dry Goods Co. Babin went on to create the finely detailed Kyle Block, one of Texas' most significant Art Deco commercial buildings. Stone and Babin had a hand in creating each of Jefferson County's outstanding public and private modernistic buildings.

Modernistic buildings can be found in most areas of Houston that were developed before 1950. The city's East End contains Houston's largest concentration of modernistic industrial buildings, constructed by companies like Ford and Hughes Tool in the vicinity of the Houston Ship Channel. Demolitions have cost Main Street most of its distinctive Art Deco storefronts, although some modernistic treasures, like Krupp & Tuffly Shoes and Sears, Roebuck & Co., may survive under slipcovers of aluminum and marble. Houston's real Art Deco gems are its small apartment buildings. Jewels like the Josephine and Almeda Court, scattered throughout the city's older residential areas, are increasingly giving way to townhome development.

Modernistic architecture turns up in unexpected places along the Texas coast. Depression-era federal programs funded the construction of new courthouses and schools in what were then small agricultural communities. Modernistic school buildings in Friendswood, Pearland and Webster still serve today's sprawling suburbs. In Baytown, Beaumont and Pasadena, the growth of the petrochemical industry fueled the construction of Art Deco and Art Moderne buildings.

Greater Houston Preservation Alliance has assembled this information to increase public awareness and appreciation of the city's surviving modernistic architecture, to focus attention on endangered buildings and provide a record of those that have been lost. This book and its accompanying Web site, *www.HoustonDeco.org,* provide a detailed sampling of the rich variety of Houston's Art Deco and Art Moderne architecture. We hope these publications will encourage readers to explore the city and discover their own examples of Houston Deco.

—David Bush
Director, Programs and Information
Greater Houston Preservation Alliance

COMMERCIAL

In 1929, shopping in Houston moved to a higher level when Sakowitz Bros. opened its specialty store on five floors of the newly completed Gulf Building. The store owners commissioned prominent "fixtures architects" Taussig & Flesch to create a completely modern retail experience. The designers crafted a richly detailed interior with floor-to-ceiling Art Deco ornamentation in each of the sales departments.

Although Taussig & Flesch designed modernistic interiors for major department stores across the United States and Canada, little remains of their work except for the restored G. Fox & Co. building in Hartford, Connecticut. Sometime after the Sakowitz store moved to a new location in 1951, the retail space in the Gulf Building was converted into offices. None of the original Sakowitz interiors survive.

Since retailers usually follow the latest fashion, it is not surprising that many commercial buildings throughout the region were built or remodeled in the modernistic style. As architectural tastes changed, Houston's Main Street lost most of its Art Deco and Art Moderne storefronts, but modernistic stores, service stations and small office buildings survive in many other older neighborhoods.

Alfred C. Finn's masterful design makes the former Gulf Building (pp. 24–26) one of the most significant examples of Art Deco architecture in the southwestern United States. In addition to housing the regional headquarters of the Gulf Oil Co., the building was home to the National

Opposite page:
Main sales floor,
Sakowitz Bros.
720 Main Street
1929
Demolished
Designers: Taussig &
Flesch (Chicago)

Bank of Commerce (now Chase), one of Houston's leading financial institutions. Finn's banking hall (p. 26) remains the city's most outstanding Art Deco public space.

Although Art Deco bank buildings are relatively rare in Texas, the Houston region possesses another outstanding example. First National Bank of Beaumont (p. 39) is at the center of that city's Orleans Street commercial district. The Kyle Block (pp. 34–35), one of the state's best examples of Art Deco retail design, anchors the north end of Orleans Street, while the White House (p. 47), a significant Art Moderne department store, anchors the south. Beaumont architect Fred C. Stone collaborated on the bank building and the department store; Louisiana native Augustin Babin worked on the Kyle Block.

Mayan relief, Petroleum Building garage

Petroleum Building
(now Great Southwest
Building)
1314 Texas Avenue
1927
Architects: Alfred C.
Bossom (New York)
with Maurice J. Sullivan
and Briscoe & Dixon

This transitional
building, inspired by
Mayan pyramids,
introduced the
stepped-back
skyscraper to Houston,
a type later refined in
the Gulf Building (pp.
24–26). The Petroleum
Building's decoration
features Mayan relief
figures, a characteristic
Art Deco use of exotic
design motifs.

23

Gulf Building
(now JPMorgan Chase Building)
712 Main Street
1929
Architects: Alfred C. Finn
with Kenneth Franzheim and
J.E.R. Carpenter (New York)

At 36 stories, the Gulf Building
was Houston's tallest skyscraper
from 1929 to 1963.

Below:
Entrance, Gulf Building

Fresco,
"Modern Houston" by
Vincent Maragliotti,
Gulf Building

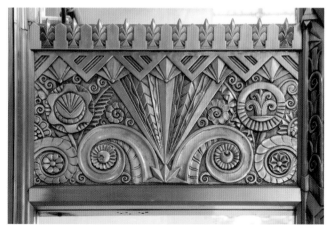

Interior metalwork, Gulf Building

Banking hall,
Gulf Building

Peden Co. Building
600 North San Jacinto Street
1929
Architect: James Ruskin Bailey

J.C. Parks Building
1201–1209 Caroline Street
1930
Architect: James Ruskin Bailey

Right:
Detail, J.C. Parks Building

Merchants & Manufacturers Building
(now University of Houston–Downtown)
1 Main Street
1930
Architect: Giesecke & Harris (Austin)

Below:
Parapet detail, Merchants & Manufacturers Building

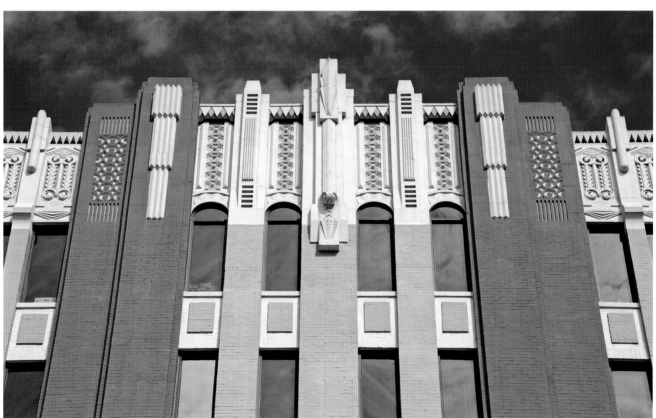

Minimax Store No. 1
1200 Westheimer Road
1930

Right:
Parapet detail, Minimax Store No. 1

HOUSTON DECO

Barker Bros. Studio
(now Lawndale
Art Center)
4912 Main Street
1931
Architect: Joseph Finger

Below:
Detail,
Barker Bros. Studio

Santa Fe Building
(now Galveston
Railroad Museum)
123 25th Street,
Galveston
1932
Architect:
E.A. Harrison (Chicago)

Galveston's railroad
passenger terminal was
completed in 1913.
The building was
greatly expanded and
remodeled with Art
Deco detailing in 1932.

Relief panels,
Santa Fe Building

Cornice detail, Santa Fe Building

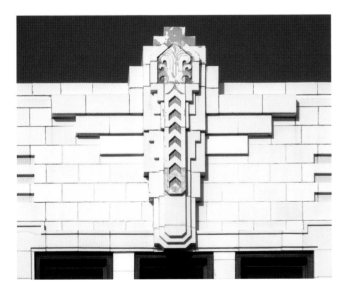

Kyle Block
207–291 Orleans Street, Beaumont
1933
Architect: Babin & Neff

The Kyle building contains 11 storefronts spanning an entire
block face in Beaumont's downtown commercial district.

Right:
Detail, central pavilion, Kyle Block

Left:
Metalwork detail,
Kyle Block

Below:
Pilaster detail,
Kyle Block

Wilson Building
1018 Prairie Avenue
1932
Architect: William Ward Watkin

Right: Grille, Wilson Building

HOUSTON DECO

Sterling Laundry
& Cleaning Co.
4819 Harrisburg
Boulevard
1935
Architect: S.R. Slaughter

Byrd's Department Store (now Byrd's Lofts)
420 Main Street
1934
Architect: Joseph Finger

First National Bank
of Beaumont
495 Orleans Street,
Beaumont
1937
Architects:
F.W. Steinman & Son
and Fred C. Stone

Relief, First National Bank of Beaumont

Flanking versions of this unusual relief are on the
upper corners of the First National Bank façade.

Below: River Oaks Community Center
2017–2047 and 2018–2048 West Gray Avenue
1937, Architects: Nunn & McGinty
with Oliver C. Winston (Washington, D.C.)

Right: Storefronts, River Oaks Community Center expansion
1953–1993 and 1952–1996 West Gray Avenue
1948, Architect: Raymond H. Brogniez

The River Oaks Community Center was one of the nation's first
auto-oriented suburban retail centers. Its unique design, with arcs
flanking either side of West Gray Avenue, was hailed as a model
for future development. One of these arcs was razed in 2007;
the rest of the complex is threatened with demolition.

Above:
Wehring's Grocery and Market
408 West Texas Avenue, Baytown
1938

Left:
Settegast Estate Building
100 West Gray Avenue
1938
Architect: Moore & Lloyd

Right:
Hawthorne & McGee Service Station
944–998 Calder Avenue,
Beaumont
1937

Below:
Kurth Building
5009–5015 Fannin Street
1940

Galveston Cotton Exchange and Board of Trade
2102 Mechanic Street, Galveston
1940
Architect: Ben Milam

Left:
Façade detail, Galveston Cotton Exchange

Above:
Knapp Chevrolet Co.
815 Houston Avenue
1941
Architects: R. Newell Walters with E. Kelly Gaffney

Right:
Peterson's Pharmacy
2439 University Boulevard
1940
Architect: Bailey Swenson

Hamman Exploration Co. (now Hobby Communications)
2131 San Felipe Road
1940
Architect: Moore & Lloyd

Mellie Esperson
Building
815 Walker Avenue
1941
Architects:
John Eberson and
Drew Eberson

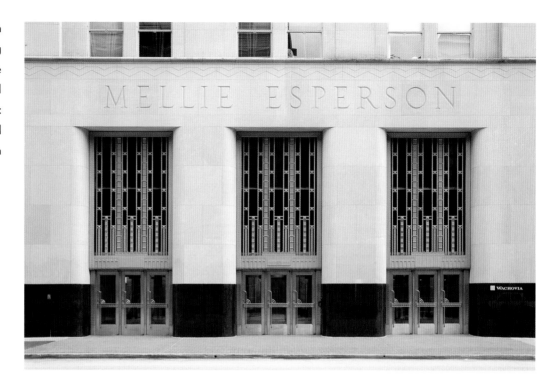

Right:
Grille, Mellie Esperson
Building

Far right:
Elevator doors, Mellie
Esperson Building

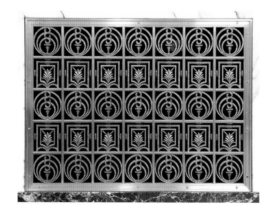

Albritton's Eats
(now La Reynera Bakery)
4120 McKinney Avenue
1945

White House Dry
Goods Co.
702 Orleans Street,
Beaumont
1942
Architect: Stone & Pitts

This department store
was completed just
before the federal
government began
rationing construction
materials as the U.S.
entered World War II.
The building now
houses Beaumont's
municipal courts.

City National Bank
Building
921 Main Street
1947
Architect: Alfred C. Finn

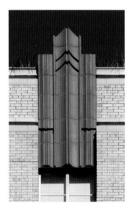

Parapet detail,
City National Bank
Building

Foley's (now Macy's)
1110 Main Street
1947
Architect: Kenneth Franzheim

Although Franzheim's revolutionary windowless design
for Foley's became the model for the modern American
department store, this transitional building also reflects
modernistic influences, particularly in its streamlined detailing.

Above:
Waples Lumber Co.
602 32nd Street, Galveston
1948

Right:
Rettig's Heap-o-Cream
210 Wayside Drive
1947

First National Bank of Goose Creek
300 West Texas Avenue, Baytown
1948
Architect: Alfred C. Finn

Lamar-River Oaks
Community Center
3256–3272
Westheimer Road
1948
Architect:
Raymond H. Brogniez

Above: Pavilion,
Lamar-River Oaks
Community Center

Sakowitz Bros. (now 1111 Main Garage)
1111 Main Street
1951
Architect: Alfred C. Finn

Left: Floral medallion, Sakowitz Bros.

HOUSTON DECO

THEATERS

The discovery of King Tutankhamen's tomb in 1922 sparked a nationwide craze that resulted in the construction of several Egyptian-themed movie theaters across the country. Egyptian Deco arrived in Houston in a big way with the opening of the Metropolitan Theater, the city's most elaborate downtown movie palace. Behind its traditional Main Street façade, the Metropolitan's ornate lobby and auditorium were encrusted with Art Deco zigzags and stylized interpretations of ancient motifs.

Art Deco and Art Moderne remained the major influences on neighborhood theater design in Houston from the 1930s through the late 1940s. Theater façades were usually a blend of modernistic styles, while Deco-inspired murals were the most popular (and affordable) form of decoration for lobbies and auditoriums. The murals in the Alabama (p. 58) and Capitan (p. 65) theaters are among the only surviving examples in the Houston area.

W. Scott Dunne of Dallas was probably the region's most prolific theater architect. Interstate Theatres, Texas' largest movie theater chain, commissioned Dunne to design many of its Houston properties, including the distinctive Alabama and Tower theaters. Sadly, much of Dunne's work has been demolished, as have all of Houston's downtown movie palaces and most of the city's historic neighborhood theaters.

Opposite page:
Metropolitan Theater
1018 Main Street
1926
Demolished: 1973
Architect: Alfred C. Finn

Tower Theater
1201 Westheimer Road
1936
Architect: W. Scott Dunne (Dallas)

Although the Tower's distinctive marquee and façade are
relatively intact, the theater's interior has been gutted.

Martini Theater
524 21st Street, Galveston
1937
Architect: W. Scott Dunne (Dallas)

Left:
Sidewalk detail, Martini Theater

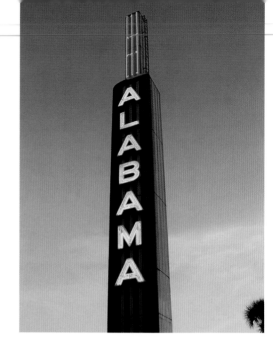

Pylon sign, Alabama Theater

In the 1980s, the Alabama's sensitive rehabilitation as a bookstore was one of Houston's first and most successful examples of adapting a historic building for a new use. Despite the successful renovation, the Alabama's owner has announced the theater will probably be demolished for mid-rise development.

Auditorium, Alabama Theater

Alabama Theater
2922 South Shepherd Drive
1939
Architect: W. Scott Dunne (Dallas)

River Oaks Theater
2009 West Gray
Avenue
1939
Architect: Pettigrew &
Worley (Dallas)

"Land" relief,
River Oaks Theater

Auditorium, River Oaks Theater

The River Oaks is the only historic movie theater in Houston that is still in operation. The theater's future is uncertain. The River Oaks' owner is considering redevelopment plans that would result in the theater's demolition.

Left: Bay Theater
3100 Market Street, Baytown
1942
Architect: Leon C. Kyburz

Below: Heights Theater
339 West 19th Street
1925
Remodeled: c. 1941

Brunson Theater
315 West Texas
Avenue, Baytown
1949
Architect:
Leon C. Kyburz

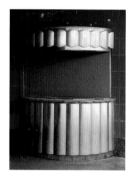

Box office,
Brunson Theater

"Shipping" relief panel, Brunson Theater

Although the Brunson's façade is largely intact,
the interior has been gutted. Designer Rudolph
Wagner created the six relief panels depicting
Baytown's major industries, which flank
the theater's sign.

Granada Theater
9231 Jensen Drive
1949
Architect:
Raymond F. Smith

The Granada and its twin, the Capitan (pp. 64–65), were built for the Isley chain, which operated theaters in Texas and Oklahoma.

Capitan Theater
1001 Shaw Avenue, Pasadena
1949
Architect: Raymond F. Smith

Mural detail, Capitan Theater

The City of Pasadena owns the Capitan
and has restored the theater's marquee
and façade. The interior remains deteriorated
and closed to the public.

Auditorium,
Capitan Theater

INSTITUTIONAL

Jefferson Davis Hospital was one of the largest public works projects completed in Houston during the 1930s. Designing the public health hospital brought together two of the city's most prominent architects: Alfred C. Finn and Joseph Finger. In addition to this collaborative effort, Finn and Finger each received important federal commissions for independent projects through the influence of Houstonian Jesse H. Jones, chairman of the federal Reconstruction Finance Corporation.

Finn designed the San Jacinto Monument (p. 78) commemorating the 1836 Battle of San Jacinto that secured Texas' independence from Mexico. After Houston's Gulf Building, the monument is Finn's most celebrated modernistic design. Finn's third major public works project was the Sam Houston Coliseum and Music Hall (1937) in downtown Houston. Both the Coliseum complex and Jefferson Davis Hospital were razed in 1999.

Finger's finely detailed Houston City Hall (pp. 80–81) is probably the architect's best known work. The municipal building is an excellent example of what is sometimes called WPA Deco, the style of many Depression-era projects financed through the federal Works Progress Administration. Exceptional courthouses in several counties surrounding Houston also exhibit this style.

Urban and rural communities also benefited from federal funding for school construction. As a result, small towns were often the sites of sophisticated modernistic buildings like Webster High School (p. 82). While most religious institutions continued to favor traditional architectural styles, a handful of congregations built modernistic houses of worship.

Opposite page:
Jefferson Davis
Hospital
1801 Allen Parkway
1937
Demolished: 1999
Architects: Alfred C. Finn
and Joseph Finger

Jefferson County
Courthouse
1149 Pearl Street,
Beaumont
1932
Architects: Fred Stone
and A. Babin

Light fixture,
Jefferson County
Courthouse

Lobby, Jefferson
County Courthouse

Detail, elevator door,
Jefferson County Courthouse

The Jefferson County Courthouse
is one of the best examples of
Art Deco architecture in Texas.
The building's ornate design sets it
apart from the more austere
WPA Deco that characterized
later Depression-era courthouses.

Alamo School
5200 Avenue N ½,
Galveston
1935
Architect:
Raymond R. Rapp

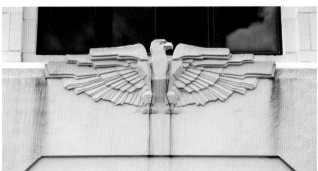

Liberty County Courthouse
1923 Sam Houston Boulevard, Liberty
1931
Architects: Corneil G. Curtis and A.E. Thomas

Left: Relief, Liberty County Courthouse

Chambers County
Courthouse
404 Washington Avenue,
Anahuac
1936
Architect:
Corneil G. Curtis

Right: Reliefs, Chambers
County Courthouse

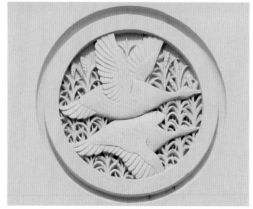

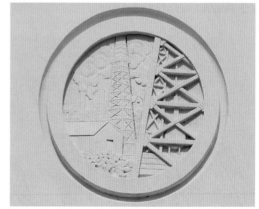

Temple of Rest, Beth Israel Cemetery
1207 West Gray Avenue
1935
Architect: Joseph Finger

The mausoleum is located in Texas' oldest Jewish cemetery, established in 1844. Joseph Finger, the building's architect, is interred within.

South County
Office Building
525 Lakeshore Drive,
Port Arthur
1936
Architects: C.L. Wignall
and Stone & Pitts

Relief, South County
Office Building

Right: Lobby ceiling,
South County Office Building

Jefferson County was the first
county in Texas to construct
a separate sub-courthouse
outside the county seat.

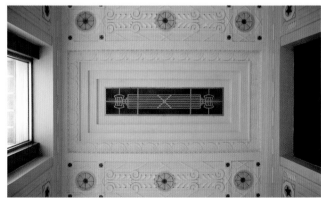

HOUSTON DECO

U.S. Post Office,
Custom House and
Courthouse
601 25th Street,
Galveston
1937
Architects: Alfred C. Finn
with Andrew Fraser
and Louis A. Simon
(Washington, D.C.)

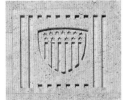

Relief, U.S. Post Office,
Galveston

Mirabeau B. Lamar Senior High School
3325 Westheimer Road
1937
Architects: Kenneth Franzheim and John F. Staub
with Lamar Q. Cato, Louis A. Glover and Harry D. Payne

Left: Houston Fire Department Station No. 11
4520 Washington Avenue
1937
Designer/contractor: J.D. Bace Corp.

Below: Orange County Courthouse
801 West Division Avenue, Orange
1937
Architect: Charles Henry Page

San Jacinto Monument
1 Monument Circle,
La Porte
1938
Architect:
Alfred C . Finn

"Building of Industries" relief by William McVey, San Jacinto Monument

South entrance, San Jacinto Monument

The monument commemorates the Battle of San Jacinto, April 21, 1836, which secured Texas' independence from Mexico.

Houston City Hall
901 Bagby Street
1939
Architect: Joseph Finger

Left: Lobby, Houston City Hall

Below: Grille, Houston City Hall

The grilles above the entrances to Houston City Hall depict lawgivers, including Hammurabi, Moses and Thomas Jefferson.

Interior signage, Houston City Hall

Webster High School (now Clear View Education Center)
400 South Walnut Street, Webster
1939
Architect: R.G. Schneider

Roy Gustav Cullen
Memorial Building
University of Houston
1939
Architect:
Lamar Q. Cato

Light fixture,
Science Building

Science Building
University of Houston
1939
Architect: Lamar Q. Cato

Right: Staircase relief, Brazoria County Courthouse

Below Left: Entrance relief, Brazoria County Courthouse

Below Right: Relief, Brazoria County Courthouse

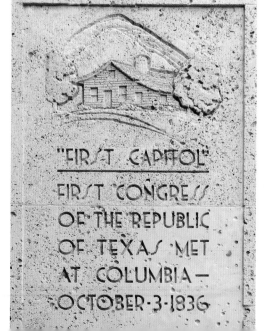

Brazoria County Courthouse

111 East Locust Street, Angleton

1941

Architect: Lamar Q. Cato

Aviation relief, Houston Municipal
Airport Terminal

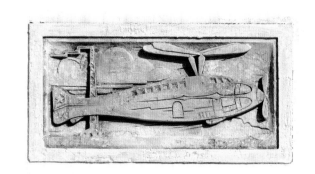

Reliefs on the terminal building
trace the evolution of air transport
in the first half of the 20th century.

Entrance detail,
Houston Municipal
Airport Terminal

Houston Municipal Airport Terminal
(now 1940 Air Terminal Museum)
8325 Travelair Street
1940
Architect: Joseph Finger

Church of Jesus Christ of Latter Day Saints
(now Metropolitan Dance Center)
1202 Calumet Street
1941
Architect: A.B. Paulson (Salt Lake City)

Sixth Church of Christ, Scientist
2202 Elgin Avenue
1941

Public School Stadium
(now Robertson
Stadium)
University of Houston
1942
Architect:
Harry D. Payne

Roy and Lillie Cullen Building
Baylor College of Medicine
1 Baylor Plaza
1948
Architect: Wyatt C. Hedrick

Left:
"Pathology" relief, Roy and Lillie Cullen Building

Ezekiel W. Cullen Building
University of Houston
1950
Architect: Alfred C. Finn

Congregation Beth Yeshurun Educational Building
(now Lucian L. Lockhart Elementary School)
3501 Southmore Avenue
1949
Architect: Finger & Rustay

HOUSTON DECO

RESIDENTIAL

The developer of the Braes Heights subdivision built this late example of modernistic residential architecture as his family home. The house's streamlined profile and wraparound windows were emblematic of Art Moderne design. The house stood for 60 years before being demolished for redevelopment.

Unlike the Houck house, most of Houston's surviving modernistic homes have angular designs reflecting the early influence of the International Style. Modernistic private homes were never common in the city, but there were several examples scattered throughout Houston. As the style fell out of favor, many of these buildings were altered to resemble more traditional houses or were demolished.

Apartment buildings and early apartment complexes exhibit some of Houston's best modernistic design. Distinctive detailing helped these buildings stand out from competing properties in the rapidly growing city. Unfortunately, many exceptional apartment buildings are being lost to new development.

Opposite page:
Residence for
Harvey R. Houck, Jr.
3780 Gramercy
Boulevard
1947
Demolished: 2007
Architect:
Harry B. Grogan

Right: Residence for Mr. & Mrs. Virgil Childress
3239 Locke Lane
1937
Architect: Moore & Lloyd

Below: Residence for Mr. & Mrs. L.D. Allen
2337 Blue Bonnet Boulevard
1937
Architect: Wirtz & Calhoun

Windsor Court
Apartments
1705 35th Street,
Galveston
1937
Architect:
Cameron Fairchild

Residence for
Dr. & Mrs. Lynn G. Howell
1601 Milford Street
1937
Architect: Campbell & Keller

Residence
1801 Lexington Street
1938

Almeda Court
Apartments
1913–1941 Prospect
Avenue
1939
Architect: Dixon & Ellis
Pictured: Courtyard,
1925 Prospect Avenue

Residence for
Mr. & Mrs. John Lroy
6748 Meadow
Lawn Drive
1939
Architect:
Harry A. Turner

Wilshire Village Apartments
1701–1717 West Alabama Street
1940
Architect: Eugene Werlin

Wilshire Village was developed as an upscale
apartment community of 17 buildings on nine
landscaped acres. Although deteriorated, the
buildings maintain a high degree of architectural
integrity. A developer has announced plans to
demolish the complex for condominium towers.

Pictured: Façade, 3816 Dunlavy Street

HOUSTON DECO

Apartments
5507-5515 San Jacinto Street
1947
Pictured: Façade,
5507 San Jacinto Street

Josephine Apartments
1744-1748
Bolsover Street
1939
Architect:
F. Perry Johnston

Duplex
1714 West Alabama Street
1947

Apartments
1901 Binz Avenue
1950

Town House Arms
Apartments
1417–1421 23rd Street,
Galveston
1948

Lobby, Town House
Arms Apartments

Hallway, Town House
Arms Apartments

INDUSTRIAL

The Carnation dairy's streamlined profile set it apart from most of Houston's angular, modernistic industrial buildings. The sharp contrast between the Carnation Company's Art Moderne styling and the classic Art Deco design of the nearby Clarke & Courts printing plant (p. 109) clearly illustrates the evolving sensibilities of architect Joseph Finger, who worked on both buildings.

The Carnation and Clarke & Courts buildings were constructed west of downtown Houston near the crafts district along Buffalo Bayou, where three large printing companies had built plants in the 1920s. Most of the city's other modernistic industrial buildings stand in and around the manufacturing district east of downtown and near the Houston Ship Channel in the East End.

Opposite page:
Carnation Company
701 Waugh Drive
1928
remodeled 1946,
expanded 1947
Demolished: 1983
Architect: Finger &
Rustay (1946, 1947)

Coca-Cola Bottling Plant
707 Live Oak Street
1926
Architects: Pringle & Smith (Atlanta) with Alfred C. Finn

Right: Medallion, Coca-Cola Bottling Plant

The plant was demolished in 2007 to make way
for a townhome development.

Dahlgren's Furniture Studio
(now Latino Learning Center)
3518–3522 Polk Avenue
1930, expanded 1940
Architect: Lamar Q. Cato
(1940 expansion)

Left:
Signage detail,
Dahlgren's Furniture Studio

Detail,
Dahlgren's
Furniture Studio

Cameron Iron Works
711 Milby Street
1935

Houston Casket Co.
1717 Live Oak Street
1935
Architect:
Moore & Lloyd

Medallion, Houston Casket Co.

Clarke & Courts Printing
& Lithography Co.
(now TriBeca Lofts)
1210 West Clay Avenue
1936
Architect:
Joseph Finger

Tower,
Clarke & Courts Printing
& Lithography Co.

Signage detail,
Clarke & Courts Printing & Lithography Co.

Above: Lone Star Creamery Co.
(now Oak Farms Dairy)
3412 Leeland Avenue
1937
Architect: J.M. Glover

Right: Parker Brothers & Co.
5303 Navigation Boulevard
1939
Architect: Joseph Finger

Hughes Tool Co., Inc.
(now Elias Ramirez State Office Building)
5425 Polk Avenue
1942

Reliefs on the building depict the self-sharpening oil well drill bit that was the source of Howard Hughes' fortune.

Left: Parapet detail, Hughes Tool Co., Inc.

Brochsteins Inc.
11530 Main Street
1940, expanded 1947
Designer: I.S. Brochstein with Lenard Gabert

The founder of this custom woodworking and furniture
company designed his firm's distinctive manufacturing plant
with assistance from architect Lenard Gabert.

Right: Signage detail, Brochsteins Inc.

Left: Ford Motor Co.
5800 Clinton Drive
1947
Architect: Giffels & Vallet (Detroit)

Below: Houston Lighting & Power Co. Eastside Substation
2501 Polk Avenue
c. 1948

HIDDEN HISTORY

Houston is often described as having no history, but much of the city's architectural heritage is hiding in plain sight. As tastes changed and styles went out of fashion, many modernistic buildings were stripped of ornamentation or "slipcovered" with marble, aluminum or stucco.

The evolution of the Krupp & Tuffly building illustrates the changes typically made to Houston's older commercial buildings. The restoration of the adjacent Smart Shop building (p. 116), which had undergone similar alterations, demonstrates the possibilities for reclaiming Houston's hidden history.

Opposite page:
Krupp & Tuffly
901 Main Street
1929
Architect: Alfred C. Finn

Façade, Krupp & Tuffly, 1953

Façade, Krupp & Tuffly, 2007

The Smart Shop (shown in 1953)
905 Main Street
1928
Architect: Alfred C. Finn

Slipcovered façade,
The Smart Shop, 1997

Restored façade,
The Smart Shop, 2006
(now Holy Cross Chapel)

Sears, Roebuck & Co.
4201 Main Street
1939
Architect: Nimmons, Carr & Wright (Chicago)

Left: Façade, Sears, Roebuck & Co., 2006

Quality Laundry
1110 West Gray Avenue
1936

Right: Parapet detail,
Quality Laundry, 2007

Far right: Façade,
Quality Laundry, 2007

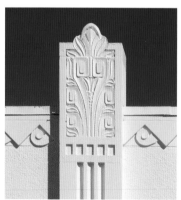

Tower Community Center
1003–1011 Westheimer Road
1937
Architect: Joseph Finger

Left: Façade, Tower Community Center, 2007

North Main Theater
3730 North Main Street
1936

Façade, North Main Theater, 2007

ACKNOWLEDGMENTS

In a project of this scope, there are many people to thank and many contributions to be recognized. We greatly appreciate the enthusiastic support and encouragement we received from Greater Houston Preservation Alliance (GHPA) Executive Director Ramona Davis from the earliest days of this project. Thanks also to GHPA's Board of Directors and President Eileen Hricik for recognizing the value of this effort and offering their support. We are very grateful to the Strake Foundation and the Houston Architecture Foundation, its Board of Directors and President Larry Whaley for underwriting this publication.

We especially want to recognize Joel Draut and the staff at the Houston Metropolitan Research Center of the Houston Public Library for their assistance and enthusiasm. Joel, in particular, was an invaluable resource whose extensive knowledge of the collections saved us countless hours of research. Ann and Jimmy Parsons contributed greatly to this project through their discoveries of hidden gems in the Research Center's photo collections and during their own travels through southeast Texas.

Our particular thanks go to Charles D. Maynard, Jr., and Jim Hudson for their advice and assistance with this project.

We are very grateful to Stephen Fox of the Anchorage Foundation for his contributions to the book. Thanks also to Brian Davis of Galveston Historical Foundation, Jeffrey Mills of the Documentary Alliance, and independent researchers Howard Perkins and David Welling for sharing their knowledge of the region's architects and architecture.

This book and its accompanying Web site, *www.HoustonDeco.org,* were made richer by the individuals who provided entry to otherwise inaccessible historic buildings: Deborah Brochstein, David Cook, Don Fischer, Greg Hassell, the Hon. William P. Hobby, Mike Isermann, Trish McDaniel, Mark McNabb, Kevin Robinson and Ed Smith.

Finally, we would like to thank Madeleine McDermott Hamm for graciously contributing the foreword to this book. Thanks, also, to Laura Baltes for providing the idea for this publication.

—Jim Parsons and David Bush

I would like to express my personal appreciation to Jim Parsons for his skill, patience and good humor throughout this process. Thanks also to David Crawford and Sally Whipple for their encouragement and support.

—David Bush

Relief map,
Lamar Senior
High School
1937

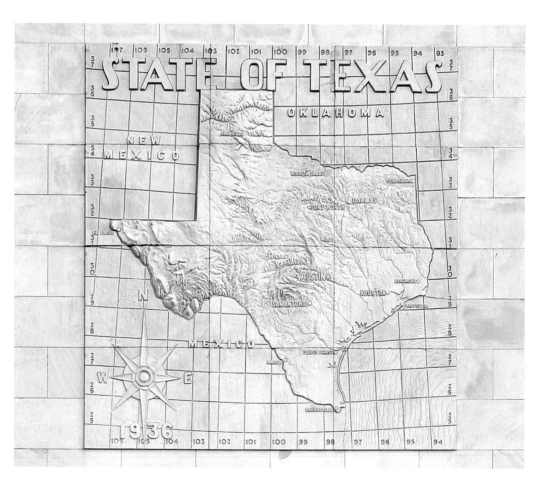

HOUSTON DECO

SELECTED BIBLIOGRAPHY

Beasley, Ellen and Stephen Fox. Galveston Architecture Guidebook. Houston: Rice University Press and Galveston Historical Foundation, 1996.

Brown, Michael E., ed. Harvin C. Moore Houston Architect. Houston Public Library/Houston Metropolitan Research Center, 1987.

Bush, David. "A Historic Preservation Plan for Beaumont, Texas." Master of Arts thesis, Middle Tennessee State University, 1995.

Fox, Stephen. Houston Architectural Guide. American Institute of Architects/Houston Chapter, 1990, 1999.

"Handbook of Texas Online." Texas State Historical Association, Austin, http://www.tsha.utexas.edu/handbook/online/.

Houston Architectural Survey, Volumes 1–6. City of Houston, 1980, 1981.

Houston Gargoyle Magazine. Various issues, 1927–1932.

Papademetriou, Peter C., ed. Houston: An Architectural Guide. American Institute of Architects/Houston Chapter, 1972.

Schmidt, Yolita. "The Moderne Style in Architecture: A Houston Guide." City! Our Urban Past, Present and Future. Houston Public Library, 1978.

Texas General Contractors Association Monthly Bulletin. Various issues, 1922–1937.

"Texas Historic Sites Atlas," Texas Historical Commission, Austin, http://atlas.thc.state.tx.us.

Wilson, Michael E., ed. Alfred C. Finn: Builder of Houston. Houston Public Library, 1983.

Writers' Program of the Work Projects Administration in the State of Texas. Houston: A History and Guide. Houston: Anson Jones Press, 1942.

Photo credits

Historic photographs

Carnation Company, Jefferson Davis Hospital, Metropolitan Theater, Quality Laundry, and Tower Community Center, courtesy of the Houston Metropolitan Research Center, Houston Public Library.

North Main Theater and Sears, Roebuck & Co. courtesy of the Bob Bailey Studio Photographic Archive, Center for American History, The University of Texas at Austin.

Krupp & Tuffly and The Smart Shop (1954) courtesy of Houston Endowment, Inc.

Sakowitz Bros. (1929) courtesy of Sikes, Jennings, Kelly.

The Smart Shop (1997) courtesy of Gensler.
Houck residence photo by Karen Lantz, AIA.

Historic postcards courtesy of the Houston
  Metropolitan Research Center, Houston
  Public Library.

Original photography

Jim Parsons—Alabama Theater, Bay Theater,
Brochsteins Inc., Brunson Theater,
Cameron Iron Works, Capitan Theater,
Chambers County Courthouse, City
National Bank Building, Clarke & Courts
Printing & Lithography Co., Coca-Cola
Bottling Plant, Congregation Beth Yeshurun
Educational Building, Ezekiel W. Cullen
Building, First National Bank of
Beaumont, First National Bank of Goose
Creek, Foley's, Ford Motor Co., Granada
Theater, Gulf Building, Hawthorne &
McGee Service Station, Houston City Hall,
Houston Lighting & Power Co. Eastside
Substation, Hughes Tool Co., Jefferson
County Courthouse, Josephine Apartments,
Knapp Chevrolet Co., Krupp & Tuffly, Kyle
Block, Lamar-River Oaks Community
Center, Liberty County Courthouse, Lone
Star Creamery Co., Lroy residence, Mellie
Esperson Building, Merchants &
Manufacturers Building, Minimax Store
No. 1, Mirabeau B. Lamar Senior High
School, Orange County Courthouse,
Parker Brothers & Co., Peden Co. Building,
Peterson's Pharmacy, Petroleum Building,
Residence—Lexington Street, Rettig's Heap-
o-Cream, River Oaks Community Center,
River Oaks Theater, Roy Gustav Cullen
Memorial Building, Roy and Lillie Cullen
Building, San Jacinto Monument, Sears,
Roebuck & Co., Smart Shop, South County
Office Building, Science Building, Temple
of Rest, Tower Community Center, Tower
Theater, Wehring's Grocery and Market,
White House Dry Goods Co., Wilshire
Village Apartments.

David Bush—Alamo School, Albritton's Eats,
Allen residence, Almeda Court
Apartments, Apartments—Binz Avenue,
Apartments—San Jacinto Street, Barker
Bros. Studio, Brazoria County
Courthouse, Byrd's Department Store,
Childress residence, Church of Jesus
Christ of Latter Day Saints, Corrigan
Center, Dahlgren's Furniture Studio,
Duplex—West Alabama Street, Heights
Theater, Hamman Exploration Co.,
Houston Casket Co., Houston Fire
Department Station No. 11, Houston
Municipal Airport Hangar and Terminal,
Howell residence, J.C. Parks Building,
Kurth Building, Martini Theater, North
Main Theater, Public School Stadium,
Quality Laundry, River Oaks Community
Center expansion, Santa Fe Building,
Settegast Estate Building, Sixth Church of
Christ, Scientist, Sterling Laundry, Town
House Arms Apartments, U.S. Post
Office—Galveston, Waples Lumber Co.,
Webster High School, Wilson Building,
Windsor Court Apartments.

INDEX

[hh] indicates that the photograph is located in the Hidden History section.